Classical Therapy

How Greek philosophy can change your life

Graham John Wheeler

Felicla Books
London

Published in the United Kingdom in 2015 by Felicla
Books

ISBN: 978-0-9931141-3-7

ALSO BY THE SAME AUTHOR

An Introduction to Classics

Contents

Introduction

This is a book about three ancient philosophies and the advice they have to offer us about living our lives.

This is not a self-help book or a how-to guide. It is more like a menu. You can pick out those philosophies or parts of them which appeal to you – or leave them all. The choice is yours.

Philosophy in the modern world is a specialised academic discipline. It has its own language, rules and culture. Being a philosopher generally means having a university-level education in the subject, beginning with an undergraduate degree and ending with a PhD. The work products of professional philosophers – books, articles and lectures – are generally accessible only to other people within the university system. Not many ordinary people in Britain today could name a famous living philosopher; and if they could, they would probably not have read his works. At best, they might have come across some of the popular writings of A.C. Grayling or

Alain de Botton – or possibly, if they are interested in politics, Roger Scruton or Terry Eagleton. When I first studied academic philosophy, I thought it was boring and pointless (I still do, actually). What did the subject have to do with the real world?

Quite a lot, as it happens – and this is particularly true of ancient philosophy. It is very important to remember that philosophy in the ancient world was quite different from philosophy as a modern academic discipline. Apart from anything else, it was a much broader enterprise. Doing philosophy could include forays into areas as diverse as zoology, educational theory, atomic physics and spiritual mysticism. More importantly for our purposes, it had a practical orientation which seems to be lacking from much modern philosophy. Ancient thinkers put forward ideas not only about the nature of reality, but also about how life ought to be lived and how a person might go about achieving happiness.

An ancient philosopher, then, was not just a thinker. He – or occasionally she – was a cross between a teacher, a spiritual adviser and a psychotherapist. One of the philosophers whom we are about to meet, the Stoic sage

Epictetus, said: "A philosopher's school is a doctor's surgery" (*Discourses*, 3.23.30). One of his rivals, Epicurus, expressed a similar sentiment:

> Empty are the words of that philosopher who offers therapy for no human suffering. For just as there is no use in medical expertise if it does not give therapy for bodily diseases, so too there is no use in philosophy if it does not expel the suffering of the soul. (Porphyry, *To Marcella* 31; trans. A.A.Long and D.N.Sedley)

So this is a practical book rather than an academic book. When describing and explaining some philosophical doctrines, I have tended to err on the side of simplicity and ease of understanding rather than pedantic technical precision. I have skated over some things, and I have generally avoided getting bogged down in learned discussions of non-essential points. Those who are interested in learning about ancient philosophy in more detail can very easily find such things elsewhere.

INTRODUCTION

*

The history of philosophy in the Graeco-Roman world goes back hundreds of years BC. The key figure in the early development of the discipline was the Athenian teacher Socrates son of Sophroniscus (c.470 – 399 BC). Socrates was not the first Greek philosopher, but he was arguably the most influential. He was succeeded in turn as the leading thinker of the Greek world by his pupil Plato (c.428 – c.328 BC) and by Plato's own pupil Aristotle (384 – 322 BC).

The holy trinity of Socrates, Plato and Aristotle are still household names today. But in this book we are going to be looking at some schools of thought which developed *after* their time and under their influence. More specifically, we will be looking at **the Stoics, the Epicureans** and **the Sceptics**, taking each of these schools in turn. These movements became enormously influential throughout the Greek world, and they continued to flourish after the rise of the Roman Empire. They later found their way, by different routes, into the philosophical thought of later times – although that part of the story is beyond our current scope.

In the case of each of our three philosophies, I will start by sketching out the general vision of the universe offered by the school in question. I will then move on to consider the school's psychological and ethical teachings, illustrating them through a selection of ancient texts. Finally, in order to give a fully rounded picture of the school, I will discuss the criticisms that were made against it by its opponents.

The rest is up to you.

INTRODUCTION

1. The Stoics

Stoicism was perhaps the most influential philosophical movement of the ancient world. At the centre of its teachings was a powerful and extraordinary claim – the claim that *anyone can be happy*.

The Stoics did not make this claim because they had a mindlessly optimistic view of the world. They were well aware of the suffering in life, and they knew that the wise man might well encounter misfortune that was unexpected and undeserved. They did, however, believe that it was possible for a person to achieve happiness by relying on their own internal resources and by going with the flow of nature.

When you think about it, this is a remarkably liberating and empowering idea. The philosopher Seneca put it this way:

Nature has seen to it that we do not need elaborate trappings in order to live well: anyone can make himself happy. The vicissitudes of life carry little weight and do not have any great power in either direction. The wise man is neither carried away by success nor depressed by failure; for he has constantly striven to rely mostly on himself and to seek all his joys from himself. (*Consolation to Helvia*, 5.1)

In order to understand how the Stoics came to adopt this approach to life, we will need to look at their broader theories about the world and humankind's place in it. Some of their theories may seem strange and outmoded today. We need not, however, accept the whole of Stoic doctrine in order to see value in its psychological and ethical elements. The "strange" bits are useful background, if nothing else.

*

The Stoic movement took its name from a place in Athens called the Painted Colonnade (*Stoa Poikilé*). This was the site where the school's founder, Zeno (c.335 – c.263 BC), first taught his doctrines. Alongside Zeno, the central founding figures of Stoicism were two men named Cleanthes (331/0 – 232/1 BC) and Chrysippus (c.280 – c.206 BC). Unfortunately, not much of any of these men's teachings survive – only scraps embedded in the works of other writers.

Some of our most useful texts on Stoic philosophy come from a much later period, being written by Stoic and Stoic-influenced writers who were active in the era of the Roman Empire. In this chapter, we will be drawing on the writings of three such men in particular: Seneca the Younger (c.4 BC – 65 AD), Epictetus (55 – c.135 AD) and Marcus Aurelius (121 – 180 AD).

Seneca was a writer and politician of Spanish origins. He made his career in the city of Rome, where he ended up serving as the tutor of the "eccentric" Emperor Nero. His father had been a public figure before him, hence the "Younger" tag. Seneca was a generally benign influence on Nero, but in the end the young lunatic got fed up with him. Seneca was falsely accused of taking part in a treasonous plot, and Nero ordered him to commit suicide, which he duly did. As we will see, suicide played a distinctive role in Stoic philosophy.

Epictetus was the most distinctively Stoic of our three men. He was a straight-talking former slave who came from modern-day Turkey. He wrote nothing, but we are fortunate that his teachings were recorded by others, in particular his student Arrian. By contrast, Marcus Aurelius was a Roman emperor. He kept a diary, conventionally known as the *Meditations*, which seems not to have been intended for anyone's eyes but his own. It is a minor miracle that the private journal of an emperor has survived down to modern times; the philosophical calibre of the journal is an added bonus. Marcus was influenced by other Stoic thinkers, but his overall world-view was distinctively his own.

If you are interested in looking further at Stoic philosophy, all of these writers' works are available in English translation as part of modestly priced paperback series, including Penguin Classics and Oxford World Classics.

One thing should be noted at the outset. Stoicism was a large movement which embraced a large number of people living in different places over a period of hundreds of years. It was not a homogeneous bloc, and individual Stoics disagreed on various points. Moreover, some writers – including those whom we are going to draw on in this chapter – took on board influences from other philosophical schools, including anti-Stoic schools like Epicureanism.

Stoicism has continued to play a small but significant part in modern culture. Most notably, there is the University of Exeter's "Stoicism Today" initiative, which serves to introduce the Stoic way of life to modern people from outside the world of academic philosophy. Stoicism has also reared its head in venues ranging from BBC Radio 4 to popular books by writers such as William B. Irvine and Jules Evans. Out of the various attempts that have been made to revive ancient schools of philosophy, Stoicism appears to have met with the greatest measure of success.

*

Imagine that you pay a visit to a Stoic-influenced philosopher in an ancient Greek or Roman city. Imagine that you ask him to tell you, in beginner's terms, the basic principles that his school teaches about life and the universe. Once you have paid your fee for the morning's tuition, he might begin by saying something like this:

"Let us start with the basics, my friend. When you look around you, what do you see? You see *material objects*. You see many of them – of different shapes and sizes, and of different kinds. A tree; a wine jug; some mud; your tunic; your own body; the bodies of other people and animals. You see *matter*. Even when you stand in what might seem to be an empty space, you can tell that matter is there – when you feel the force of the wind blowing against your face, for instance.

"So we live in a *material* universe. Now, we have no reason to say that the material universe is endless in size. The matter must surely end somewhere. If you were to look at the universe from the outside, we may presume that you would see a limited body of matter surrounded by infinite space. Nevertheless, as we are human beings and we live in these worldly surroundings, matter is the first thing that we see and feel around us.

"But that can't be all there is. Matter by itself is a lifeless thing. Matter by itself is like that stone – passive, inert, cold. The stone sits where it is, dull and shapeless, slowly being worn away by the rain. You can pick it up and throw it; but soon it will fall to rest again.

"Is the universe nothing more than a large chunk of stone? Of course not. Pure matter may be lifeless and inert, but just look around you – the universe is neither of those things. It is *filled* with life. The matter which we see all about us does not sit there like that stone. It *moves*. It has shape. It has order. The universe is a great collection of pieces which fit together like the pieces of a child's toy, and which move in endless harmonies – from the men, plants and animals that live on the earth, to the tides and the seasons with their familiar patterns, to the sun and the stars which move in their constant cycles around us.

"There must be something which *pervades* the matter – something which sets it in motion and gives it order and structure. What we call that something is mostly, perhaps, a matter of taste. Are you a pious man, my friend? If so, you might call it 'God' or 'Zeus'. Or are you one of those men who dare to think strange new thoughts about such matters? If so, then just call it 'Nature'.

"Whatever you wish to call it, it is a reality, and just as real as matter. It is the binding principle which holds the universe together and makes it what it is. The universe is not just a stone or a collection of stones. It is an intricate web in which everything is connected to everything else. A single, united whole – its body being matter and its soul being God or Nature. For the world itself has a soul, and the souls of men are tiny fragments of it. And it is in order to take care of your soul, I think, that you are paying me so generously to teach you."

This was the universe that the Stoics lived in. It was a material universe, but one which was pervaded by what might variously be called God, Nature, or – to take another term that was frequently used in this context – the principle of "Reason" (*Logos* in Greek). Such ideas will be unfamiliar to many people today. They must not be confused with the idea of a creator god, which may be more familiar to us from the Judaeo-Christian tradition – a deity who creates and governs the world but in some sense sits outside or above it. The Stoics were pantheists. God was in everything. God *was* everything.

What's more, Stoicism taught that everything in the world is linked together and that events are connected by endless chains of causation which stretch off into the past and the future. The different parts of the universe simultaneously both go about their own business and interact together with each other, like cogs in an enormous, elaborate machine. This vision of the cosmos, in which nothing is random and everything is connected to everything else, meant that Stoicism developed what some might call a fatalistic streak. There is a story that, when the Stoic founding father Zeno beat his slave for stealing, the slave argued that he had been fated to steal. "And also to be beaten", replied the philosopher. Ho ho.

The fatalistic streak in Stoicism has important implications for its teachings about how human beings ought to behave. If everything is linked together and pervaded by a transcendent principle of God or Nature, there isn't really much point in trying to kick against the pricks. We don't make our own luck and we can't fight our fate, so it's best just to accept it. Stoic philosophy accordingly taught that people should roll with the punches of life. The enlightened Stoic will look upon the ups and downs of the human condition in the same way as the ebbing and flowing of the tides. He will accept them in a spirit of resignation.

These ideas are absolutely central to Stoicism, so it is worth taking some time to quote what sources have to say about them. Marcus Aurelius expressed a classic Stoic mindset when he wrote:

> Whatever happens to you was destined for you from eternity. The web of causes has eternally woven your existence together with this event. (10.6)

He went on to apply this principle, in typically Stoic fashion, as a means of discouraging attachments to external things:

The well-schooled and modest man says to Nature, who gives everything and takes it away: "Give what you wish, take away what you wish." (10.14)

Epictetus had already used this same metaphor of Nature periodically giving things to us and then taking them back. He even applied it to one of the worst experiences that life has to offer, the loss of a loved one:

Never say of anything, "I lost it", but rather, "I gave it back". Your child has died? You gave him back. Your wife has died? You gave her back. "My property has been confiscated." No, you gave that back as well. (*Enchiridion*, 11)

In a longer passage, Epictetus recommends that the attitude with which we face what life offers us – and what it fails to offer us – should be like that of a guest at a symposium, or ancient Greek dinner party:

Remember that you ought to behave as if you were at a symposium. Something is brought round to you: put out your hand and take it with dignity. Something passes you by: don't snatch at it. Something has not yet come to you: don't let your desire get ahead of itself, but wait until it reaches you. Behave in this way in respect of children, a wife, power and wealth, and you will be worthy of dining with the gods. And if you go further and refrain from taking what is offered to you, then you will not only share in the gods' banquets but also in their supremacy. (*Enchiridion*, 15)

That final reference to refraining from taking things highlights that asceticism formed part of the Stoic life. We will come back to this point.

It is also worth hearing from Seneca. As a courtier of an emperor, Seneca was a wealthy and powerful man. But he was well enough versed in Stoic philosophy – and understood well enough that his boss was a psycho – to realise that it was a bad idea to take his good luck for granted:

> I have never trusted in Fortune, even when she seemed to be favourable to me. All those things which she generously bestowed on me – money, honours, influence – I put in a place where I could retrieve them without troubling myself. I have kept a great gulf between myself and them; and so Fortune has lifted them from me rather than torn them away. Fortune can menace no-one with her enmity if she has not first deceived him with success. (*Consolation to Helvia*, 5.4)

Seneca also had what looks like the same hard-hearted attitude to bereavement as Epictetus. He wrote the following words as part of an essay to console a woman for the loss of her son:

> If you mourn for the death of your son, you are condemning the hour in which he was born; for his death was laid down for him at his birth. He

was born subject to this law; this fate attended him all the way from the womb. We are born under the rule of Fortune, which is hard and unconquerable, and we shall suffer things both deserved and undeserved according to her will. (*Consolation to Marcia*, 10.5)

The Stoics' ordered, fatalistic view of the universe had other consequences too. For example, it included a cyclical view of time. Stoic philosophers taught that the world went through eternally repeating cycles. These involved periodic destructions of the whole universe by fire, followed by endless rebirths. On a less exalted level, another consequence of the deterministic Stoic conception of the world was that Stoics believed in the reality of divination. After all, if everything in the universe happens in accordance with fixed patterns of causation, it must in principle be possible to predict the future.

It is perhaps worth emphasising at this point that Stoicism was not a religion. In spite of their distinctive teachings on the cosmos, metaphysics and ethics, Stoics would not have considered themselves to be members of a different religion from the other ancient Greeks and Romans. They continued to participate in the traditional rituals of classical paganism, even though their ideas were somewhat different from traditional popular beliefs. They might, for example, see the individual gods of the ancient pantheons as aspects of the ultimate ineffable God. Some Stoic texts seem sincerely pious, which is why they often went down well with later Christian readers. Cleanthes, for example, composed this typically Stoic prayer:

> Lead me, O Zeus, and you, O Destiny,
> on whatever path you have set out for me.
> I will follow without delay....

Yet the Stoics were quite religiously unorthodox in other ways. Zeno, for example, disagreed with building temples to the gods. A mere work of builders and craftsmen could not, he said, be of any real value or sacredness. Moreover, in spite of Cleanthes' fine words, it was recognised that prayer had its limits. Epictetus, who was one of the more "religious" Stoics, counselled his followers not to rely on divine intervention to solve their problems:

> We say: "Lord God, may I no longer be anxious." Idiot – haven't you got hands? Didn't God give them to you? You might as well kneel down and pray that your nose doesn't run. You'd do better to wipe it and leave the prayer. (*Discourses*, 2.16.13)

*

A key theme in Greek philosophy is the *telos* – the "end" or "objective". Not unnaturally, philosophers thought that part of their task was to uncover the *telos* of human life, in much the same way as Monty Python or Deep Thought in *The Hitchhiker's Guide to the Galaxy*. Philosophers from Aristotle onwards came up with the answer that the *telos* of humanity is something called *eudaimonia*.

The word *eudaimonia* is generally translated into English as "happiness". This is a good enough translation, but the word means something broader and deeper than just feeling generally good about how things are going. Aristotle said that it consists of what makes life desirable and complete. In the light of what we have learnt so far about the Stoic world view, it should come as no surprise that the Stoic founder Zeno taught that *eudaimonia* meant "to live in agreement with Nature". In order to be happy in the truest sense, we must align ourselves with the governing principle that pervades the material world. As we have also seen, this can be framed in different ways. In secular terms, it means that the rational mind must align itself with the Reason that corresponds with the workings of the universe. In spiritual terms, it means that the soul must live in harmony with God. This is how Marcus Aurelius put it:

> Everything which is in harmony with you, O Universe, is in harmony with me. Nothing which is in good time for you is early or late for me. Everything which your seasons bring, O Nature, is a crop for me. Everything is from you, everything is in you, everything goes back to you. (4.23)

At this point, some of the more distinctive and challenging features of Stoicism begin to kick in. For a Stoic, living in harmony with Nature and Reason means living in accordance with the faculty of reason that we possess as human beings. We must live *rationally*. After all, argued the Stoics, reason is the special gift that Nature has given to us, the one that sets us apart from other animals. From this perspective, to be fully rational is to achieve our *telos* as human beings and to attain *eudaimonia*. The philosopher Diogenes of Babylon summed up the essence of Stoicism when he said that the *telos* of human life is to act rationally in choosing those things which are in accordance with Nature. When you think about it, these are pretty strong claims, and perhaps surprising ones. They amount to an assertion that reason – and not, say, love, spirituality or achievement – is the true key to happiness. It is the sort of thinking that Mr Spock might approve of.

If we have followed our lesson in Stoicism up to this point, we can now go on to make some more specific value judgements. We can identify what is *good*, or virtuous. Something is good and virtuous if it brings us to our *telos* of rationally living in accordance with Nature, which in turn means *eudaimonia*. This way of thinking is the source of one particular claim that the Stoics became famous for: the claim that happiness consists in virtue.

The Stoics taught that there are four primary virtues from which all the others flow: prudence, courage, temperance and justice. (They got this theory of the four primary virtues from Plato – it later ended up influencing Christian moral thinking.) There was a corresponding set of vices – imprudence, cowardice, and so on. Being committed to an impeccably rational view of things, the Stoics defined the virtues as forms of *knowledge*. Prudence, for example, is the knowledge of what is good, what is bad and what is neither. To be virtuous is not just to obey a set of moral rules, it is to *know how to live*.

These ideas have some consequences which at first sight may seem rather odd. First, as Seneca points out, if happiness depends on rational judgement, then stupid people can never be counted as happy. They can no more achieve *eudaimonia* than can rocks or animals – the problem in each case being a lack of reason. Another consequence, which is noted by Epictetus, is that "bad" people – robbers and the like – are merely *mistaken*. They should not be condemned, but rather offered pity and a rational explanation of the truth. Punishing someone with a deficient faculty for moral reasoning is like executing someone for being blind or deaf.

There is a further important consequence of Stoic thinking on values and virtues. Something is only good or virtuous for a person if it represents a rational choice which he has made, one which is aligned with the workings of the universe. Likewise, things which are bad or which amount to vices are the product of people making defective choices. It follows that something can only be good or bad if it *lies within our power* – if it is something about which we can make a choice. If something is outside our power, we ought not to engage in any value judgements about it. It is an "indifferent" – a concept which we will come on to shortly. Epictetus made this point with typical bluntness:

"A man's son has died."
The answer: "It is outside his control. It is nothing bad."

"A man's father has died and left him nothing."
What do you think? "It is outside his control. It
is nothing bad."
"Caesar has condemned him to death."
"It is outside his control. It is nothing bad."
"He grieved over these things."
"That is in his control, and it is bad."
"He bore them with dignity."
"That is in his control, and it is good."
(*Discourses*, 3.8.2-3)

Not worrying about things that are outside our
control means, quite apart from anything else, not
worrying about how other human beings are behaving.
When Epictetus was asked to stop a man's brother from
being angry with him, he replied: "Bring him to me and I
will talk to him – but I have nothing to say to you about
this other man's anger" (*Discourses*, 1.15.5).   Marcus
Aurelius put the point succinctly:

It is ridiculous not to flee our own wrongdoing, which we *can* do, but to attempt to flee that of others, which we *cannot* do. (7.71)

So much for Stoic rationality and its consequences. If reason is the Stoic's friend, emotion is his enemy. Zeno defined emotion as a movement of the soul which is contrary to reason and to Nature. The desires of a true Stoic ought to be under rational control. More than that – they ought to be rational in themselves. Emotions pose a threat to the studied reasonableness that should characterise the Stoic way of life. They stop a person from achieving his fulfilment or *telos*. They get in the way of happiness.

The Stoics defined the main emotions as grief, fear, desire and pleasure. They regarded them as being essentially errors of judgement, just as they regarded the virtues as consisting of correct knowledge. Avarice, for example, is the irrational misjudgement that money is a good in itself. The Stoic life did not extend even to what we might consider to be quite harmless emotions. We are told that the Stoic sage will not even feel wonder when presented with something extraordinary like a volcanic eruption.

Love has always been seen by philosophers as something of a problem because it tends to overpower the rational mind. The ultra-rationalistic Stoics naturally shared this prejudice. They accepted love in the sense of friendship, but they taught that sexual passion should be avoided. Epictetus even compared the experience of being in love to slavery – and for a former slave like him this was more than just a cheap metaphor. It is said that Zeno pointedly got up and walked away from Chremonides, a young man whom he was attracted to. When asked why, he replied that good doctors say that the best cure for inflammation is rest.

The Stoics' aversion to emotion was not utterly rigid. It was nuanced in a couple of ways. The Stoics realised on some level that a complete absence of emotions might not be such a good thing. A man without emotions would not necessarily be a virtuous sage. Sociopaths existed in the ancient world just as they do in ours, and the Stoics knew that they didn't want to end up like them. The Stoics were also reluctantly prepared to recognise what might be termed "good" emotions. There were three of these: joy, caution and wishing. They were, respectively, the rational counterparts of pleasure, fear and desire. Zeno probably allowed himself to *wish* to be friends with Chremonides even if he fought against the *desire* to sleep with him.

The practical effects of Stoic ideas about virtue manifested themselves in different ways. Consistently with what we have already seen, they encouraged what we might call a passive approach to life. The wise person will accept with rational serenity whatever fate brings. He will not shut himself away and refuse to get out of bed, but he will not show an excess of energy and enthusiasm either. As Marcus Aurelius put it:

> This is what one's character will do if it is set for its *telos*: live out every day as if it were its last, never being agitated, never being torpid and never engaging in pretence. (7.69)

Yet the Stoic life of virtue can also be seen in a rather different way, as something that demands hard-edged, unbending effort. If good, virtuous Stoic behaviour is the only aim of life and the only route to happiness, the true sage will give himself over to it totally. This is what Marcus said what he was in this sort of mood:

> Whatever anyone does or says, I must be good. In the same way, an emerald (or gold, or purple) might constantly say: "Whatever anyone does or says, I must be an emerald and keep my colour."
> (7.15)

This vision of the Stoic life is characterised not by serene passivity but by uncompromising commitment.

*

Living a life which is good and virtuous sounds fine in theory. But, as we all know, not everything in life can simply be labelled "good" or "bad". The Stoics accordingly recognised a large class of things which they termed "indifferents". These "indifferents" included attributes such as health, poverty, beauty, pain and reputation. Such things were classified as indifferents because, according to the Stoics, they do not bring happiness or unhappiness in and of themselves. They do not inherently benefit or harm a person; and they can be put to both good and bad uses.

The Stoics weren't soft in the head, and they realised very well that not all indifferents are equal. Some, such as health, are clearly "preferred", while others, such as poverty, are "rejected". The preferred indifferents are by no means to be confused with true virtues. But they can at least be seen as being in accordance with Nature, and they can contribute indirectly to right living. Seneca wrote:

> The wise man does not consider himself unworthy of any of the gifts of Fortune. He does not love wealth, but he does prefer it. He does not take it into his soul, but he does take it into his house. He does not reject the wealth he possesses, but retains it and wants it to supply greater material for his virtue. (*On the Happy Life*, 21.4)

Nevertheless, giving too much importance to indifferents of any kind is foolish, or even dangerous. If a person comes to believe that his interests are bound up with indifferents, then those indifferents will become a competing claim on his care and attention. He will come to neglect the true virtues. This is just wrong-headed. After all, the gods are happy without external accoutrements, so why do *we* need them?

What's more, if we get hung up on indifferents, we end up giving control of our lives to other people. As Epictetus said: "In general, attributing value to something which is external puts you under somebody else's control." (*Discourses*, 4.4.1) He elsewhere elaborated on this theme:

....[H]e who has a desire or an aversion for things which are not within his power can be neither faithful nor free, but is forced to shift around and suffer being inflamed... and he is forced to be obedient to other people who have the power to give or deny those things to him. (*Discourses*, 1.4.19)

This idea that the Stoic sage will be unattached to indifferents which lie in other people's gift is the other side of the coin to the doctrine that only things which are within our own rational control are good or bad.

It is a characteristic of indifferents that they are fragile. They are given to us only conditionally. Seneca, who was painfully aware that his wealth and status were dependent on the whims of a tyrant, knew this better than most. He offered this advice:

> Whatever shining gifts have fallen to us, Marcia – children, honours, wealth, big houses... a famous name, a well-born or beautiful wife, and all the other things which are dependent on the uncertainty and fickleness of chance – they are adornments which are borrowed and do not belong to us. None of them is given to us as a gift. The stage of life is decorated with props which are borrowed and must be returned to their owners. Some of them will be returned on the first day, others on the second day, and a few will

remain right to the end. (*Consolation to Marcia*, 10.1)

This harks back to the idea which we met earlier that losing things is just a matter of giving them back to the universe.

One mistake which we must especially be on our guard against is getting truly bad things confused with things that are merely "rejected" indifferents. This principle gave the Stoics an answer to the age-old problem of why good people experience suffering. Seneca wrote:

"Why does God allow bad things to happen to good men?" In fact, he allows no such thing. He keeps all bad things away from them – crimes, disgraceful acts, dishonourable thoughts, avaricious plans, blind lust and greed which menaces others. He protects them and rescues them from such things. Surely no-one will ask this too from God, that he looks after their *luggage* as well. (*On Providence*, 6.1)

In similar vein, Epictetus said that complaining about a bad man prospering was like pointing out that a man who had gone blind still had his fingernails intact.

Regarding external things as indifferents made for a way of life that had a decidedly ascetic streak. The principle of asceticism recommended itself even to a wealthy courtier like Seneca:

> Let us get used to disregarding outward show and taking account of the usefulness of things, not their attractiveness. Let food take care of hunger and drink of thirst; let lust flow where it needs to. Let us learn to rely on our own bodies and conform our dress and food not to the latest fashions but to the customs of our ancestors. Let us learn to increase moderation, curb luxury, restrain arrogance, soften anger, look calmly on poverty, cultivate frugality... and seek for riches from ourselves rather than from Fortune. (*On Tranquility of Mind*, 9.2)

Epictetus, who was less rich than Seneca, had this to say on the matter:

> As far as the body is concerned, take only what you need, as far as food, drink, clothing, accommodation and slaves are concerned. Cut out anything which is meant for show or meant to impress people. (*Enchiridon*, 33.7)

> The body is the proper measure of what possessions each person needs, just as the foot is for one's shoe. If you are faithful to this principle, you will keep to the proper measure; if you go beyond it, you will inevitably be carried away, as if you were falling off a cliff. It is the same with a shoe – if you go beyond what the foot needs, you will come to buy shoes that are gilded, then purple, then studded with jewels.... (*Enchiridion*, 39)

On the other hand, it should be said that the Stoics were not masochists. They did not make asceticism an end in itself, and they realised that it could be taken too far. Indeed, it could result in failing to observe the key Stoic precept to live in accordance with Nature. As Seneca said:

> Our business is to live in accordance with Nature, and it is against Nature to torment one's body, to hate basic cleanliness, to seek out squalor and to eat food that is not merely cheap but disgusting and horrible..... Philosophy requires frugality, not punishment; and frugality need not be drab. (*Moral Letters*, 1.5.4-5)

One of the most difficult doctrines of Stoicism is the notion that life itself is an indifferent. This means that, in some circumstances, suicide becomes a viable option. This might be the case where, for example, virtue is no longer possible; where one is severely ill or in pain; or where one's death would benefit one's friends or country. The classic case of Stoic suicide was that of the Roman statesman Cato the Younger, who stabbed himself when he was defeated by Julius Caesar in one of Rome's civil wars. In later years, as we mentioned earlier, Seneca received an order from the Emperor Nero to commit suicide. He calmly obeyed it, realising that the game was up. This gives an added poignancy to his written reflections on the subject:

> As you know, life is not always to be clung on to. It is not living that is a good thing, but living well. So the wise man will live for as long as he needs to, not as long as he can. He will foresee where he is going to live, with whom, how and what he is going to do. He always considers what kind of life he has, not how long it will be. (*Moral Letters*, 8.1.4-5)

There was no Stoic party line on what happened *after* death. Some Stoics thought that all souls continued to exist until the next cyclical destruction of the world by fire. Others thought that only the souls of wise men were durable enough to survive death. Marcus Aurelius just didn't know, and didn't care that much either:

The man who is afraid of death is afraid either of not experiencing anything or of experiencing something new. But either you will experience no sensation and therefore nothing bad; or else you will have a new kind of sensation and you will be a different kind of being, but you will not stop being alive. (8.58)

In any event, the sting of death was diminished for the Stoic by the knowledge of what an insignificant part of the world he was. "Soon you will forget everything. Soon everything will forget you." (7.21) That was how Marcus Aurelius reconciled himself to his fate. It is striking that even a Roman emperor could tell himself how utterly negligible he was and how laughably small his realms were:

First, do not be troubled; for everything is in accordance with the nature of the universe. And in a short time you will be nothing and nowhere, just like [the Emperors] Hadrian and Augustus. (8.5)

Asia and Europe are corners of the universe. The whole ocean is a drop in the universe.... Everything that exists at the present time is a point in eternity. Everything is small, changeable and disappearing. (6.36)

Seneca said much the same thing:

Count up the time allotted to cities: you will see for how short a time even those with a reputation for being very old have stood. All human affairs are brief and fragile, and count for nothing in eternity. If we compare it with the universe, this earth with its cities, its people, its rivers and the expanse of its oceans appears no larger than a speck; and our existence is smaller than a speck.... (*Consolation to Marcia*, 21.1-2)

*

By this point, you may be able to see how modern English has developed the colloquial sense of "Stoic" as someone who keeps a stiff upper lip in the face of bad luck. And, indeed, the figure of the Stoic sage as a man of granite who stands unbowed before the slings and arrows of fortune was certainly known to the ancient writers:

> There is no doubt that whoever has succeeded in scorning those who provoke him has raised his head above the common herd and stands at a higher level. It is a feature of true greatness not to feel a blow. In this way does a great beast calmly turn to face barking dogs; in this way do the waves uselessly beat against a vast rock. (*On Anger*, 3.25.3)

But I hope you can also see that there is much more to the Stoic philosophy of life than being able to hold on to one's dignity when the chips are down. What Stoicism offers is nothing less than the chance to live a life of rationality and happiness. What is more, it offers the chance to be *free*. Only the Stoic sage can act with true freedom and independence – seeing the world as it really is, making free and rational choices, pursuing the *telos* of life. The unenlightened man, by contrast, will make the wrong judgements and will end up living beholden to others.

This, of course, is a particular vision of happiness. It is the view that happiness consists not of getting what you want, but of being free from being troubled by things that trouble most other people. Getting what you want is transitory. Even if you manage to avoid losing your possessions, suffering bereavement or falling ill, there is always Death waiting at the end to laugh at your pretensions. Stoicism can't bring you good luck – no philosophy can do that. But it does claim to able to do something which may be even more valuable: it can teach you how to handle *bad* luck. It can teach you the right *attitude*. Here is Epictetus again:

> What if someone grabs me by the cloak and drags me to the town square, and people shout at me: "What good have your teachings done you, philosopher? See, you're being dragged off to prison and you're going to be beheaded." But what kind of philosophical training could I have

taken to prevent a stronger man from seizing me by the cloak and dragging me off?... I have learned nothing except for this: I understand that whatever happens that is outside my choice is nothing to me. (*Dialogues*, 1.29.22-24)

The journey to this kind of Stoic serenity starts from within. A key part of becoming free from common human troubles is becoming free from our own perverse and misleading ideas about things. External misfortunes will only frighten or depress the Stoic if she falls prey to accepting wrong judgements about them – and, being perfectly rational and clear-sighted, she will not make that mistake. Unlike the rest of us, she will not allow herself to be a prisoner of mistaken thought patterns that chance to intrude into her head. Understanding the importance of our own thoughts and seeing them for what they really are – that, for a Stoic, is the beginning of wisdom.

This is a crucially important point, and one which we can illustrate richly from our ancient sources. It was understood particularly well by Marcus Aurelius. He kept returning to the subject in his diary:

If you are grieved at something outside of yourself, it is not the thing itself that troubles you, but your judgement on it – and you can take that away immediately. But if you are grieved at something within your own character, who is stopping you from setting the offending part right? (8.47)

Remove the thought and the fact of being harmed is removed. Remove "I am harmed" and the harm is removed. (4.7)

The deeds of men are not what annoy us, but rather our opinions of them..... Take the opinions away and be willing to refrain from judging something to be a disaster, and your anger is gone. (11.18.7)

Remember that everything is what you think of it. (2.15)

Here is the same idea from Epictetus:

It is not things which disturb human beings, but their opinions of those things. For example, death is nothing terrible... but the opinion that death is terrible, *that* is terrible. Whenever we are held bound or troubled or feel depressed, let us never blame anything other than ourselves – that is, our opinions about the matters in question. (*Enchiridion*, 5)

For Seneca, this approach provided another source of consolation for the death of a loved one. We might miss living friends who happen to be away from us, but we do not mourn for them; and this is so even though, objectively speaking, they are just as physically absent as the dead. Seneca concluded from this that mourning is based on something intrinsic to our own thoughts:

The one who mourns is assailed by desire for the one who is absent. But it appears that this desire is tolerable in itself: for we do not weep for those who are absent or are going to be absent while they are still alive, although all contact with them is taken away from us along with the sight of them. It is opinion, therefore, which tortures us; and every evil is as great as we judge it to be. (*Consolation to Marcia*, 19.1)

These ideas are uncannily similar to the ideas promoted by modern psychologists in Cognitive Behavioural Therapy or CBT. One of the central principles of CBT is that our feelings are driven by our thoughts, so changing our thoughts will result in changing our feelings. This similarity with ancient Stoicism is no accident. Albert Ellis and Aaron Beck, the pioneers of CBT, were explicitly influenced by the Stoics – and the crossover continues today. For example, Stoicism is at the forefront of the work of Donald Robertson, a psychologist and writer who specialises in CBT.

The Stoics also seem to have used practical techniques which resemble certain types of modern therapy. For example, Marcus Aurelius advocated managing one's thought patterns by constantly driving certain thoughts into one's mind – rather like mantras or affirmations. This would lead to a general change in mental outlook:

> Your state of mind will be in line with such things as you are accustomed to think, for your soul is dyed by your thoughts. So dye it with continual thoughts of this sort: "Wherever you can live, you can live well".... (5.16)

For his part, Seneca advocated a form of practical therapy. He set aside time each night to scrutinise his conduct during the day. In this way, he made himself constantly accountable as he strove for self-improvement.

*

As we have noted, Stoicism is a philosophy of life which continues to be attractive to a significant number of people today. But it also contains some apparent flaws, and we will end this chapter by discussing these.

Some people would flatly deny the central metaphysical claim of Stoicism. What if the universe just *isn't* pervaded by anything? What if the material world *is* inherently cold, random and meaningless? This objection essentially amounts to an assertion of a rather robust form of atheistic materialism. A discussion of it is beyond the scope of this book, save insofar as it links in with Epicureanism, the next philosophy which we will be looking at. Nevertheless, it is worth remembering that Stoicism doesn't necessarily demand any great leaps of faith – the minimum required is acceptance of a kind of vague principle of Nature or fate. And, as we said at the start of this chapter, it is possible to value the psychological and ethical insights of Stoicism – such as the principle of acting without attachment to indifferents – without necessarily accepting all of its broader claims.

Other claims made by the Stoics seem rather extreme – and, indeed, they were seen as extreme even in ancient times. Is rational virtue *really* the only thing that is needed for happiness? The essayist Plutarch, whose sympathies were with Plato's school, asked sarcastically whether the Stoic would be happy when stretching out a finger prudently, or when being tortured prudently, or when rationally breaking his neck. In the same vein, our ancient sources contain stories about Stoics who failed to walk the walk. King Antigonus told the philosopher Persaeus that his property had been ravaged by enemy soldiers. When Persaeus' face fell, Antigonus commented that this showed that wealth was not in fact an indifferent. The philosopher Dionysius defected from Stoicism because he suffered from a severe eye infection and he was no longer prepared to claim that pain was an indifferent.

How far such criticisms have force depends on how far one buys into the concept of happiness as freedom from external attachments. This version of the good life is not for everyone, nor even perhaps for most people. It was uncongenial even to some Stoics. There *were* Stoics who were prepapared to walk the walk, even at personal costs which ranged up to and including suicide. Yet some other members of the school lost their nerve and conceded that rational virtue alone was not enough. Happiness also required good health and some level of material livelihood. The philosopher Chrysippus made another, slightly unusual concession. A Stoic wise man who achieved public office, he said, would behave *as if* wealth, honour and health were true goods.

Talk of public office raises another issue. The passivity that seems to be central to Stoicism might appear to be incompatible with taking part in public affairs and trying to change the world for the better. What would have happened if, say, Nelson Mandela or Martin Luther King had adopted a path of unemotionally flowing with the tides of the universe?

The best response to this criticism is to point out that Stoicism *has* consistently attracted people with public roles and responsibilities. A whole series of Roman politicians were practising Stoics, including Cato the Younger (the one who stabbed himself), Marcus Junius Brutus (the one who stabbed Julius Caesar) and of course our friends Seneca and Marcus Aurelius. Later fans of Stoicism have included King Frederick the Great of Prussia, George Washington and (perhaps a little surprisingly) Bill Clinton. Modern followers of Stoicism in the business world include Jonathan Newhouse of Condé Nast and Carrie Sheffield of *Forbes* magazine.

Going back to the charge of extremism, the Stoics made various other claims that seem difficult to swallow. They claimed that all of the virtues are interlinked and that every virtue is equal. It follows that a person who has one virtue has them all. Accordingly, the Stoic wise man was supposed to behave perfectly and to be free from all error. Chrysippus went so far as to claim that the Stoic sage is as good as Zeus. It is a wonder that he was not incinerated by a thunderbolt on the spot.

The other side of the coin is that all vices are also the same, and are equally bad. One lie is just as untrue as another. Everyone who is not a Stoic is a complete idiot, and it is idle to distinguish degrees of idiocy. After all, a drowning man is still drowning, whether he is deep in the ocean or just under the surface. Non-Stoics were also described by Stoics as lunatics, as slaves and as enemies to each other.

Quite understandably, this sort of talk got the Stoics a reputation for arrogance. There were reports of Stoics making a point of refusing to speak to the unenlightened – while at the same time being willing to invest their money with them, vote for them at elections and marry their daughters to them. Not many people today would want to emulate the Stoics in these respects.

Finally, the exalted role that Stoicism assigns to reason can be seen as a serious stumbling block. The Stoics' claims on this subject don't seem especially plausible in psychological terms. They arguably had to cheat: they included in their definition of rational behaviour things which we would characterise as being essentially emotional – honouring one's parents, for example, and being loyal to one's country. They also, as we have seen, ended up accepting a kind of limited role for emotions.

Part of the problem with the Stoics' obsession with reason was that they looked upon the human mind as consisting *only* of a rational faculty. Irrationality was just a misuse of this faculty, an error of judgement. Stoicism had no room for the notion of a complementarity between rational and irrational parts of the psyche, each of which has a valid and necessary role to play. Yet most of us experience precisely this duality on a daily basis.

THE STOICS

2. The Epicureans

An epicure dining at Crewe
Found quite a large mouse in his stew.
Said the waiter, "Don't shout
And wave it about,
Or the rest will be wanting one too."

In modern English, an "epicure" is a gourmet: a connoisseur of fine food and wine. The term has a long history. It goes back to the Epicurean movement of ancient Greece – and it is that movement which is the subject of this chapter. As we will see, the meaning of the term has changed a great deal over the centuries. The original Epicureans would be very surprised to find themselves classified with the likes of A.A. Gill and Michael Winner.

The Epicureans were followers of the philosopher Epicurus (341 – 270 BC). Epicurus was an Athenian by descent and spent much of his adult life in Athens. The term "epicure" in English originates from the fact that Epicurus based his teachings on the pursuit of pleasure. But Epicurus was not an epicure. He did not equate "pleasure" with wining and dining, or any other form of sensual indulgence. On the contrary, the Epicurean philosophy had something of an ascetic streak. Nevertheless, misinterpretations of Epicurus and his teachings have been around since ancient times. Even in antiquity there were rumours along the lines that he consorted with prostitutes and that he vomited twice a day from over-indulgence.

So the modern equivalent of the Epicurean would not be Michael Winner. It would, if anything, be Richard Dawkins. The spiritual heir of Epicurus is the enlightened man who seeks to free himself from irrational fears and superstitions through hard-headed scientific realism. Epicurus' followers saw him as a hero who had taken on the lies and oppressions of religion and won:

> When humanity was lying supine, in open disgrace,
>
> crushed throughout the world under the weight of
>
> Religion...

it was a man from Greece who first dared to raise up

his head in opposition and first offered resistance;

the myths of the gods did not daunt him, nor their
    thunderbolts,

nor the grimly thundering sky; no, instead he was

provoked to greater boldness as he strove to break

open the tightly closed doors of nature for the first time.

His blazing power of mind won out, and he journeyed off,

far beyond the fiery ramparts of the heavens;

he travelled all through the universe in his mind and
    spirit....

So now Religion in turn lies vanquished and crushed
    under

our feet, and our victory raises us up to the skies.
    (Lucretius, 1.62-79)

An important concept in Epicurean thought was
physiologia, or natural science. The Epicureans even put
forward something resembling the theory of evolution.
More generally, they claimed that humanity's hope lay in
cultivating an understanding of the natural world. This in

turn would lead the way to a life of pleasure, as opposed to one of avoidable suffering. A famous Epicurean text put it like this:

> I declare that the vain fear of death and that of the gods grip many of us, and that joy of real value is generated not by theatres... and baths and perfumes and ointments, which we have left to the masses, but by natural science.... (Diogenes of Oenoanda, fragment 2; tr. Martin Ferguson Smith)

Epicureanism had some resemblance to Stoicism insofar as it was interested in nature and taught that humans should live in accordance with nature. Epicurus himself wrote a treatise entitled *On Nature*. The Epicureans also shared with the Stoics a healthy respect for rationality and reason. But the ethos of the two movements is quite different, and they were perceived as rivals even in antiquity. Epicureanism lacks the transcendent, metaphysical dimension of Stoicism; and, more importantly, it is designed to solve different problems and fits with a different character type.

Our sources for Epicureanism are a little less accessible than our sources for Stoicism. This isn't necessarily a problem, as Epicureanism seems to have been a more conservative sort of movement. Its teachings didn't change as much with the passage of time as those of its rival. Most of Epicurus' own works have perished, but we have some letters that were said to have been written by him. These may be genuine, although it is difficult to be certain that they all are. We have the remains of a long inscription from the second century AD which was set up by an Epicurean called Diogenes in his home town of Oenoanda (in modern-day Turkey). Most oddly of all, we have a heap of papyrus scrolls dug up from the ancient town of Herculaneum, which was buried under volcanic lava by the eruption of Vesuvius in 79 AD. These scrolls were first discovered in 1754 in a villa which seems to have belonged to the Roman politician Lucius Calpurnius Piso Caesoninus. It is believed that they were assembled by an associate of his, the Epicurean philosopher Philodemus. The texts have yet to be fully transcribed, but they are currently being examined by scholars with the assistance of modern technology.

The outstanding source for Epicurean teaching, however, is a poem entitled *On the Nature of Things (De Rerum Natura)* by Epicurus' Roman disciple Lucretius. This poem is a lengthy explanation of the Epicurean view of the world, as well as being a considerable piece of literature in its own right. We will be drawing quite a bit on Lucretius as a source in this chapter: for example, the quotation above about Epicurus' victory over religion comes from near the beginning of his poem. Many English translations of Lucretius are available, both in prose and verse, for anyone who wants to explore his work further. Be warned, however: it can be a little dry at times.

Epicureanism has been revived in the modern era, albeit on a rather smaller scale than Stoicism. The American founding father Thomas Jefferson was an avowed Epicurean. Today, there are a few resources available for those with an interest in the philosophy, such as newepicurean.com, epicurus.net and the Society of

Friends of Epicurus. Epicureanism is also discussed in popular books such as Jules Evans' *Philosophy for Life*.

*

The Epicureans' basic methodology was solidly empirical. They held that our knowledge of the world comes from our senses. Our senses can be trusted to tell us the truth about things.

This is not a particularly remarkable idea. More surprising is the fact that the key concept in Epicurean science was something which, although undoubtedly real, is not perceptible to the senses at all – the atom. The idea that everything is made of tiny elementary particles – *atomoi*, or "indivisible things" – was not invented by Epicurus. It went back to two earlier Greek philosophers, Leucippus (5th century BC) and Democritus (460 – 370 BC). The ancient Greek theory of atoms fed directly into modern atomic physics, and it was superseded only as recently as the 19th century, with the advent of subatomic theory – although the Epicureans could claim to have pioneered subatomic physics too. They accepted that atoms could be considered as being composed of smaller units, even if they could not be physically split up into those units.

The Epicureans believed that everything consists of either matter or space – atoms or "void". There is no third option. As for the atoms, they exist eternally and they are infinite in number. One consequence of this is that there exists an infinite number of worlds:

> We must not think that it is at all likely –
> as the infinite void of space gapes open on every side
> and limitless masses of atoms of endless number
> fly about in all directions in eternal motion –
> that this is the only earth and sky in existence....
> ....We must acknowledge
> that there are other worlds elsewhere in the universe,
> and different races of men and kinds of beasts.
> (Lucretius, 2.1052-56, 1074-76)

No "things" exist other than matter composed of atoms – there are no spirits. The Epicureans believed that a human soul existed, but they meant by this something closer to the physical brain than to a spiritual entity. The

Epicureans' "soul" was composed of matter; it consisted of particularly fine atoms located mainly in the chest area (they hadn't yet worked out that we do our thinking with our heads).

The Epicureans theorised that we can see, hear and smell things because objects give off tiny quantities of the atoms which they are made of, rather like a fire gives off heat. These tiny quantities of atoms travel through the air and strike our sense organs, or, in some cases, the mind itself – this is how, for example, we are able to dream. Sometimes the flows of atoms can become mixed up, leading to false ideas. For example, the idea of centaurs – the mythical creatures which were half-horse and half-human – originated when the flows of atoms given off by horses and humans got mixed up and ended up causing confusion in people's minds.

It might seem as if the Epicureans, with their atom-based materialism, saw the world as being fundamentally mechanistic and predictable. But Epicurus hated the fatalistic streak he saw in Stoicism and rejected that kind of thinking. For the Epicureans, the universe was a rather unpredictable sort of place. Whereas Democritus had seem his atoms as individual parts in an enormous machine, the Epicureans allowed space for randomness and free will. They did this by positing that atoms experience tiny deviations in their movement through the void – the famous theory of "the swerve". The theory of the swerve was enough to liberate their universe from the chains of mechanistic determinism. It is also vaguely reminiscent of some of the claims of modern quantum physics about the essential indeterminacy of the universe at its deepest level.

Unlike most other ancient Greeks and Romans, the Epicureans were unconcerned about the gods. Note that Epicurus did not *deny* the existence of the gods. To that extent, he was not a fully-fledged Dawkinsian. Epicureans were sometimes accused by their opponents of being straightforwardly godless, but this was probably not quite correct. The Epicureans were faced with the stark fact that all peoples have *some* form of religion and *some* ideas about divine, supernatural powers. Given the importance that their philosophy attributed to perceptions, they felt bound to concede that people's ideas of the gods meant that the gods were in some sense real. Quite how far this concession went is still being debated by scholars. The most likely interpretation is that the Epicureans believed that the perceptions of gods which we have in our minds are accurate perceptions which originate from atoms given off by some genuine entities somewhere in the universe.

On a practical level, Epicurus encouraged his followers to participate in the traditional ceremonies of Greek religion, rather like an atheist fellow attending Sunday evensong in an Oxbridge college. He seems to have had no interest in behaving like an iconoclast. He was not, however, religious in any meaningful sense of the word. Yes, the gods existed in some sense, but they had no interest in human affairs. Nor did they create the world. It's not as if the world we live in is a particularly well-designed place. And, after all, if matter is eternal and infinite, it makes no sense to speak of anyone creating anything. In any case, *why* would the gods have done such a thing? No, the gods have nothing to do with us. If they live anywhere, they must live far away in eternal bliss. We can't blame them for things that happen here. Thunder, for example, is caused by physical phenomena in the atmosphere, not by Zeus being angry – not that Zeus *would* be angry, according to the Epicurean view. Most ancient Greeks thought of the gods as being characterised by human weaknesses, but Epicurus disliked that sort of thinking. It was ideas like that, he argued, that were truly impious – not his philosophical theories.

As for human society, the Epicureans taught that humans had originally lived in an uncivilised state of nature and had gradually built up civilised society from there. They regarded civilisation with some ambivalence. For all its obvious advantages, it had led to an increase in problematic desires and in conflict. Even the greatest achievement of human civilisation – the rule of law – was a mixed blessing. On the one hand, it is useful insofar as it stops us (mostly) from killing each other. On the other hand, it poses a potential threat because it entails fear of punishment for wrongdoing – and eliminating fear, as we shall see, was a big deal for Epicureans.

*

Let's back up a bit for a moment. We saw in the last chapter that a key concern of Greek philosophy was finding out the aim, or *telos*, of human life. We also saw that, not surprisingly, it was widely agreed that the *telos* of human life is *eudaimonia*, which is loosely translated as "happiness".

We are now in a position to start unpacking the central claim of Epicurean philosophy: that happiness lies in pleasure. The Epicureans taught that there are two states of feeling, pleasure (*hédoné*, from where we get "hedonism") and pain. We are, by nature, drawn to pleasure and repelled by pain. We have a natural affinity to pleasure – it is *fitting* for us. Pain, on the other hand, is our enemy. To be happy is to maximise our pleasure and to minimise our pain. This is the fundamental objective of life. Everything else is secondary and subordinate. Being virtuous, for example, is only a means of attaining the ultimate aim of pleasure. The Epicureans compared the virtues to medicine which a man takes in order to achieve the objective of good health. The Stoic philosopher Cleanthes had his own way of satirising this viewpoint:

He told his listeners to join him in imagining a painting of Pleasure. She is decked out in beautiful clothing and queenly accoutrements, and is seated on a throne. The Virtues are on hand as her slave-girls, and they do nothing and carry out no duty other than to minister to Pleasure and to whisper in her ear... that she should take care not to do anything imprudent which might offend the minds of men or anything from which any pain might arise. "We Virtues are born to serve you, and we have no other task." (Cicero, *De Finibus* 2.69)

Pausing there, it might seem at first sight that we don't need any philosophical guidance in order to attain happiness. The Epicureans appear to have done themselves out of a job. If happiness consists in pleasure and pleasure is something that we are naturally drawn to, why can we not become happy by simply following our instincts? The Epicurean answer would be that our rational mind has a role in all this too. We are capable of making errors of judgement. Yes, we must follow our inborn instincts to maximise pleasure and minimise pain, but we must be smart about how we do so – and being smart requires a knowledge of Epicurean philosophy. All pleasures are good, but in some cases the process of obtaining a particular pleasure means that it is not worth the cost. Moreover, it is sometimes necessary to practise deferred gratification and to accept a certain amount of pain as the price for receiving a greater pleasure at some point down the line. By contrast, the crude and immediate pleasures sought by the sensual man do not truly free him from pain.

The Epicureans fundamentally believed that they had discovered something that most pleasure-seeking people hadn't. This could lead to a certain amount of smugness. Lucretius wrote, in a famous passage:

> How sweet, when the great waters of the sea are
>   churned by winds,
>
> to watch from dry land another man desperately
>   struggling....

This is pretty blatant *Schadenfreude*, but it is only fair to note that Lucretius immediately added a caveat:

> ....not because we are well pleased that someone is
> in trouble,
>
> but because it is sweet to see the woes that we are
> free from. (Lucretius, 2.1-4)

Part of what set the Epicureans apart from the pleasure-seeking multitude was their distinctive definition of pleasure. The Epicureans believed that pleasure is, in its purest form, something *negative*. It is the *absence* of pain:

> The outer limit of pleasure is the removal of all
> pain. (Sovran Maxims, 3)

The most blessed condition for a human being is a combination of an absence of pain in the body and an absence of disturbance in the soul. The absence of disturbance in the soul was regarded as especially important: for Epicurus, psychological pleasure was the best sort. It was known by the Greek term *ataraxia*, which means something like "not-being-hassled". People who don't grasp these ideas and chase after obvious forms of gratification are missing the point:

> They do battle in intellect, they compete in rank,
> spending their nights and days in relentless effort
> to reach and conquer the heights of wealth and power.
> What miserable minds these men have, what blind
>   hearts!
> In what shadows they live, amidst what dangers
> they spend this paltry little life! Do they not see
> that nature cries out for nothing for herself, save that
> pain stays away from the body and that the mind enjoys
> pleasant feelings, far removed from worry and fear?
>   (Lucretius, 2.11-19)

The key to the Epicurean version of happiness was therefore to make rational choices with a view to achieving the absence of physical pain and the ultimate mental pleasure of *ataraxia*. This was the purpose of life. As Epicurus is said to have put it:

The man who has a firm understanding of these things will know how to direct every choice, positive and negative, towards the health of the body and the *ataraxia* of the soul, as this is the *telos* of a happy life. For everything that we do is for the sake of avoiding pain and fear. (Diogenes Laertius, 10.128)

And again, this time emphasising the distinction between true Epicurean pleasure and sensualistic hedonism:

A pleasant life does not come from endless drinking and revelry, nor from indulgence with women and boys, nor from fish and all the other things which form part of a lavish table, but from sober reasoning, working out the grounds for every choice, positive and negative, and driving out those opinions through which the greatest disturbance takes hold of the soul. (Diogenes Laertius, 10.132)

If pleasure is primarily mental, so also is pain. The main sort of pain which the Epicureans were concerned about was fear. Some fears are legitimate, but others are not. In particular, the wise man will overcome any fear of death and of punishment in the afterlife. Epicurus' materialistic philosophy allowed him to say with confidence that there *is* no afterlife. The soul is mortal, and it cannot survive once the body has ceased to function. Death is nothing more or less than the dissolution of the atoms that make up the human person. For Epicurus, figuring this out was a life-changing breakthrough:

> There is nothing terrible in life to the man who has properly understood that there is nothing terrible in ceasing to live. (Diogenes Laertius, 10.125)

> Death is nothing to us. What has decomposed has no feeling, and what has no feeling is nothing to us. (Sovran Maxims, 2)

The correct attitude towards death was to accept it with calm realism. This, for example, is the advice that Lucretius gave to his readers:

> Certain it is that an end to life is laid down for mortals.
> We cannot avoid our doom: we must go to meet it....
> By extending our life, we cannot take a scrap of time
> away from our death, nor are we able to pluck
> a single moment from the long ages of our decease.
> (3.1078-1089)

As passages like these might indicate, it would not be much of an exaggeration to say that the whole system of Epicurean philosophy was an elaborate means of providing relief from the fear of death.

Let us return from fear and pain to the more congenial subject of pleasure. It will perhaps be clear from what we have said so far that the best pleasures are passive, or "static" in the jargon, rather than active or "dynamic". The obvious sensual pleasures sought by hedonists are "dynamic". Epicurus did not by any means reject dynamic pleasures, but he was aware of their limits. They are not enough. They are inextricably linked with feeling a lack of something and hence an unfulfilled desire. Eating fine food, for example, consists of satisfying the appetite. For an Epicurean, desire is something to be regarded with suspicion. Some desires are natural or necessary – for example, our desires for happiness, comfort or life itself. Others, however, are "empty". These would include the desire for such things as immortality or wealth. This leads to an important Epicurean insight or paradox. Empty desires are the hardest to satisfy – indeed, desire for something like immortality is *impossible* to satisfy. It follows from this that choosing to walk the Epicurean path to happiness is an *easier* option than simply going along with the general herd of humankind. Lucretius put it succinctly: "Life on earth is a Hell for fools" (3.1023).

Perhaps the most notorious example of the Epicureans valuing static over dynamic pleasures is their contrasting attitudes towards friendship on the one hand and sexual love on the other. For an Epicurean, friendship is extremely important. It arose out of necessity as society was evolving, but it has become a source of pleasure. It involves a deep empathy and a profound level of commitment: the Epicurean wise man might even be prepared to die for the sake of a friend. As for sex, however, it is never worth the trouble, and indeed it generally carries a net cost. The wise man will probably not get married, and he will certainly not fall in love. In a famous and mean-spirited passage, Lucretius mocked the irrational blinding effect that love has on the lover.:

> The discoloured girl is *honey-brown*; the smelly dirtbag,
>   *unkempt*;
> the grey-eyed one, *like Athena*; the scrawny one, *a*
>   *gazelle*;
> the dwarf, *utterly charming, one of the Graces*;
> the great big one, *stunning, a real lady*;
> the stammering one's *got a lisp*, the tongue-tied one is
>   *modest*;
> the nasty bitch who talks too much is *a great laugh*;
> the one who's emaciated and half-dead is *lovely*
> *and slim*; the one with terminal TB is *delicate*;
> the one with outsize breasts is *like Ceres nursing Bacchus*;
> the pug-nosed one's *a Satyress*, the blubber-lipped one's
>   *great to kiss*. (4.1160-1169)

A modern reader might be forgiven for thinking that Lucretius' real problem was not with irrational emotionalism but with women, full stop.

Lucretius also had some other ideas in this area which might seem rather challenging. If love is the enemy, we need an effective defence against it. Lucretius thought that this was to be found in promiscuity. Whatever you do, he advised, when your girlfriend is away, don't keep thinking about her. Sleep with other girls instead:

> It is good to flee those images, and frighten off
> whatever nourishes your love, and turn your mind
>   elsewhere,
> and cast your stored-up seed into other bodies;
> rather than retain it, bound by the love of one woman,
> and save up worry and certain pain for yourself.
> For the ulcer grows and takes root as it is nourished,
> the madness increases each day and the woe grows
>   heavier –
> unless you combat the wounds you have with new blows,
> and quickly cure them by freely seeking sex from all
>   quarters.... (4.1063-1071)

Another, rather different example of the practical implications of Epicureanism was the tendency that Epicureans had to avoid what would have been seen as the duties and responsibilities of citizenship. Epicurus himself did not go into public life, and his followers tended to take the same course and avoid anything to do with politics or civic affairs. This was of a piece with their dislike of competing over what were thought to be empty honours. This explains why Epicureanism could be severely criticised by a man like the Roman statesman and amateur philosopher Cicero, who devoted his life to public service. None of this means that Epicureans were antisocial or that they rejected prevailing laws and customs. On the contrary, they taught that a wise man will obey the laws of his state. The stated reason for doing this, however, was that being a bad citizen unnecessarily exposes a person to punishment – and an Epicurean can do without that kind of risk and the fear that goes with it. Epicureans did not see civic-mindedness as a virtue in itself.

The upshot of all this is that the Epicurean lifestyle could be rather ascetic – surprisingly similar to the Stoic way of life, in fact. Epicurus had this to say:

> Simple food brings the same pleasure as an expensive diet, once the pain of hunger is removed; and barley-cake and water provide the greatest pleasure when they are brought to someone who is hungry. (Diogenes Laertius, 10.130-131)

Lucretius put it more succinctly:

> If a man guides his life using right reason,
> he will find vast riches through living on little,
> with a serene mind; for little is never in short supply.
>   (5.1117-1119)

Another feature which Epicureanism shared with Stoicism is the idea that managing our thoughts is the key:

> What causes hunger is not the stomach, as most people think, but rather the false opinion that the

stomach needs endlessly to be filled. (Vatican Sayings, 59)

Also on the subject of therapeutic ideas, we find the interesting notion that an Epicurean should interrogate his own desires. A rational process of self-questioning and reflection will allow us to get our priorities in order:

> Put this question to each of your desires: "What will happen to me if what this desire is seeking is achieved, and what will happen if it is not achieved?" (Vatican Sayings, 71)

On the whole, however, the Epicureans were less interested in psychology than the Stoics. They did not emphasise the task of reprogramming our inner thoughts. They don't give us a proto-manifesto for CBT.

*

We have hopefully said enough by now to sketch out the main lines of the Epicurean view of the world. The time has come to briefly review some criticisms that might be made of the Epicureans' approach to life.

To begin with, the behaviour of the ancient Epicureans might seem somewhat offputting to modern people. If the Stoics were arrogant, the Epicureans were cultish. Epicurus founded a distinct community (which, usually, included women), located near Athens and known as "the Garden". After his death, his followers venerated him with something approaching a personality cult. There is an element of this in Lucretius' work, which contains repeated paeans of praise to him. The Epicureans even held celebrations on the twentieth day of each month to commemorate Epicurus and his associate Metrodorus, a practice which the great man himself had apparently mandated in his will. They became known as the "Twentiers" as a result.

Modern Epicureans are not, of course, required to replicate this sort of thing. But there are perhaps more fundamental difficulties raised by Epicurean philosophy. One of the strongest selling points of Epicureanism in the modern world is its scientific, secular ethos. For many people, this will be entirely to its credit. There is no shortage of people who would be willing to cheer Lucretius on as he blasts away at the iniquities of religion. For many others, however, this approach to life and the universe will come across as reductive and one-dimensional. There isn't much room in Epicurean philosophy for anything other than a strictly materialistic view of existence – and materialism is certainly not to everyone's taste. Not only is Epicureanism difficult to reconcile with traditional forms of religious belief, which is enough in itself for many people to reject it. It is also incompatible with more modest claims, such as the idea that human life has a spiritual dimension and the notion that the universe embraces both the natural and the supernatural.

This leads us on to another point. As has been indicated, Epicureanism looks very much like a system whose fundamental purpose is to take away the fear of death, and perhaps also fear of the gods. This, for example, is how the great Roman epic poet Virgil chose to sum up the achievements of Lucretius:

Happy was he who was able to know the causes of
  things,
and who crushed every fear, our ineluctable fate,
and the roar of merciless Acheron beneath his feet.
(*Georgics*, 2.490-492)

Acheron was one of the rivers of the Underworld in Greek mythology.

The difficulty here is that most people in modern Western society tend to spend little time worrying about either death or religion. Some people do. Maybe everybody does at some time. But we live in an age which, rightly or wrongly, likes to keep death shut safely behind the doors of hospitals and religion behind the doors of churches; and which does not share the ideas about eternal punishment that were prevalent in previous times. If anything, modern people are more likely to be disturbed and depressed by the ideas that there are no gods and that death is the end. Seen from this angle, Epicureanism is redundant. It is a solution in search of a problem.

Finally, Epicurean theories about the nature of pleasure and happiness might strike us as being unconvincing. Some of us might conclude that Epicurus was simply wrong that hedonism is a bad idea. There doesn't, after all, seem to be any shortage of people who take the view that booze, sex and gluttony are jolly good things. Such people might be more comfortable with the philosophy of the Cyrenaics, who opposed the Epicureans in ancient times for this very reason. On the other hand, the Cyrenaics did not fare well: they ended up being pretty thoroughly eclipsed by the Epicureans, which is why we talk about "epicures" today rather than "cyrenes". Epicureanism won the battle of ideas because it seems to have been regarded as a more satisfying approach to life – at least among the intellectual types who interested themselves in such philosophical debates.

More fundamentally, Epicurus' conception of happiness is one that is likely to appeal mainly to a particular kind of personality. Some of us may have no difficulty in relating to the idea that happiness is something essentially static rather than dynamic. But, clearly, not everybody feels this way. Whether or not you like the sound of Epicurus' theories may depend on whether you prefer to lie in bed all day watching Youtube videos or get up and hit the gym or the shops. For many people, *ataraxia* may seem worryingly close to boredom.

THE EPICUREANS

3. The Sceptics

The last school of philosophical thought that we will be looking at is perhaps the most difficult and challenging of all.

We might be tempted to assume that we know what a Sceptic is. After all, "sceptic" – or "skeptic" in American English – is a common English word. And there is no shortage of people who are happy to assume it as a label. There are Skeptics Societies, *Skeptic Magazine*, the *Skeptical Inquirer* and even Skeptics in the Pub. Everyone knows what a Sceptic is – don't they?

Not necessarily. Ancient Sceptics were different. In modern society, the term has mostly been colonised by people with fairly specific philosophical convictions: essentially, people with a liking for scientistic rationalism. Judging from their writings and speeches, their scepticism tends to be quite selective. In practice, it is mostly confined to religion and the supernatural; and, to a lesser extent, minority beliefs from popular culture like UFOs and homeopathy. A self-describing sceptic in the modern world is likely to have fairly robust convictions in other areas of life. But the ancient Sceptics were much more radical. They were not rationalists; they saw no reason to confine their scepticism to religion or popular beliefs; and their general ethos was agnostic rather than atheistic. They doubted *everything*. Modern sceptics – with the exception of some academic philosophers like Jonathan Barnes – tend not to do that.

As it happens, the "Sceptic" label is not entirely accurate. *"Sképsis"* in ancient Greek meant "inquiry". A Sceptic was therefore someone who was engaged in the business of inquiry. The Sceptics were sometimes also known as "Zetetics", which meant much the same thing ("Searchers"). But such descriptions are misleading. Scepticism as a philosophy was not about feeding a thirst for knowledge. The Sceptics had no expectation of making new discoveries that would increase the level of human understanding of the world. If anything, the reverse was the case. They would have actively *resisted* the claim that someone – anyone – had come across some new insight or discovery. Their interest was not in clarifying but in blurring. It is said that, while on an embassy to Rome, the Sceptic philosopher Carneades shocked people by arguing in favour of justice one day and against justice the next. These guys were interested in showing people how much they *didn't* know.

The keynote of Scepticism, then, was not *inquiry*. Nor, for that matter, was it exactly *doubt*, although that comes closer to the mark. It was *indifference*. This was reflected in other ancient words which were used to describe members of the Sceptic movement: "Ephectic", which means "he who suspends judgement", and "Aporetic", which means "undecided". When faced with a claim about how things are, the Sceptic neither accepted nor rejected it, but instead suspended judgement. That was the central feature – the essence – of what Scepticism was. It was summed up by the Sceptics themselves in a series of pithy slogans which included the following:

"I suspend judgement"

"We determine nothing"

"Nothing is preferred"

"Every argument has an opposing argument"

The Sceptics saw themselves as different from the other philosophical schools of the ancient world, including the Stoics and the Epicureans. Members of the other schools made it their business to assert and mount arguments in favour of specific claims about the world. This was the antithesis of Scepticism. The Sceptics accordingly referred to all other philosophers with the blanket term "Dogmatists". The other philosophers in turn didn't spare the Sceptics from searching criticism. Lucretius, for example, scarcely bothered to hide his contempt:

> If someone thinks that nothing is known – he does not
> know
> that *that* can be known, since he declares that nothing is
> known.
> I disdain to pursue a debate with such a man,
> who has put his head where his feet ought to be.
> (4.469-472)

Broadly speaking, there were two distinct camps of Sceptics in antiquity, the Academic Sceptics and the Pyrrhonian Sceptics. There is some scholarly debate about precisely how and to what extent these camps differed, and for present purposes we will have to talk in slightly crude generalities. The Academic Sceptics considered themselves to be the successors of the philosophical founding father Socrates, who had made a point of approaching every question in a spirit of critical analysis. Academic Scepticism is so called because in the course of the 3rd century BC it came to be the official house line of the famous Academy in Athens, the institution founded by Socrates' pupil Plato.

In summary, the Academic Sceptics fell into the obvious trap of claiming that it is a certain principle that there are no certain principles. This was the very contradiction that invited Lucretius' riposte above. A claim that nothing can be known is, after all, a claim of knowledge. We can, if we like, brush this off as an trivial paradox – rather like the truism that a free society should tolerate everything except intolerance, or Obi-Wan Kenobi's absolutist claim that only a Sith deals in absolutes. In ancient philosophical discourse, however, this inconsistency was regarded as a serious flaw, not only by Dogmatists like Lucretius but also by other Sceptics.

In this chapter, we will mainly be focusing on the second camp of Sceptics, the Pyrrhonian Sceptics. Adherents of the Pyrrhonian tendency sought to escape from the logical bind that afflicted the Academic Sceptics. They declined to make the claim that we need to be sceptical about everything. They acknowledged that such a claim might itself be false, and they adopted a similar attitude towards the Sceptical slogans that we referred to above. So, for example, the catchphrase "We know nothing" was to be interpreted as meaning "We know nothing, *not even this*". For the Pyrrhonians, even the tenets of Scepticism itself were to be regarded sceptically, and Sceptical statements that sounded like absolutes were not to be taken at full strength or face value. The Pyrrhonians were so radically sceptical that they labelled the Academic Sceptics as "Dogmatists" or "Stoics" on occasion.

Pyrrhonian Scepticism is named for Pyrrho of Elis (c.370 – c.272 BC), a former painter who gained a reputation for following an ultra-sceptical philosophical path. Pyrrho himself, however, wrote nothing and founded no school. The earliest Pyrrhonian Sceptic who put pen to papyrus was a fellow called Timon of Phlius, who lived some years later (c.320 – c.230 BC). Some of his musings still survive today. This was his take on things:

> ....Timon says that the man who means to be happy must look to these three things: first, what are the natural qualities of things; secondly, in what way we should be disposed towards them; and lastly, what advantage there will be to those who are so disposed.
>
> The things themselves then, he professes to show, are equally indifferent, and unstable, and indeterminate, and therefore neither our senses nor our opinions are either true or false. For this reason then we must not trust them, but be without opinions, and without bias, and without wavering, saying of every single thing that it no

more is than is not, or both is and is not, or neither is nor is not.

To those indeed who are thus disposed the result, Timon says, will be first speechlessness, and then imperturbability....

(Eusebius, *Praeparatio Evangelica*, 14.18 (trans. E.H. Gifford))

The reference to "imperturbability" is significant. The underlying Greek word is *ataraxia*, the same term that the Epicureans used for the serene state of not-being-hassled. We will come back to this point.

Pyrrho's doctrine was revived – not entirely in its original form, it seems – in the first century BC by Aenesidemus, a lapsed Academic Sceptic. The largest body of Pyrrhonist writings which survives today consists of the work of a doctor known as Sextus Empiricus. Sextus was active in the 3rd century AD, by which time Scepticism was already in decline. English translations of his works can be found in several modern series, including Cambridge Texts in the History of Philosophy and Clarendon Later Ancient Philosophers.

*

One fundamental reason for the division between the Sceptics and the Dogmatists was that the Sceptics recognised no "criterion of truth". That is, they did not accept that there is any way of determining what is real and what isn't. They held that we can rely neither on our senses nor on our reason to tell us the truth.

As we saw in the last chapter, the Epicureans thought that we could trust our senses. Our senses, they argued, are able to detect and inform us about the characteristics of other material objects by virtue of the tiny streams of atoms which those objects give off. The Stoics had their own theory about the "criterion of truth", which seems slightly odd to a modern reader and which can be no more than summarised here. They thought that we can know what is true if we receive something called a "grasping appearance" (*phantasia kataléptiké*). A grasping appearance is an accurate representation of reality, and when we receive one we can safely accept it. This obviously raises the question of how we can know when we are receiving one of these grasping appearances.

After all, even very convincing appearances can be deceptive. There is a story that the Stoic philosopher Sphaerus was tricked into thinking that realistic-looking fake pomegranates made out of wax were the real thing. The Sceptics also pointed out that a dream might seem highly realistic until one wakes up.

For a Sceptic, the key point is that there is no way of establishing a criterion of truth. Our perceptions of how the world is are inconsistent and open to dispute. If we try to probe further in an effort to achieve a greater degree of certainty, we end up with the opposite result. Sooner or later, we come to realise that the task is impossible – whereupon we throw up our hands and achieve a kind of inner peace.

This leads us on to a point of crucial importance. As indicated by the passage quoted above from Timon of Phlius, the goal or *telos* of Scepticism was to obtain *ataraxia*. There is an important similarity here with Epicureanism, but also an important difference. Unlike the Epicureans, the Sceptics thought that *ataraxia* consisted not in pleasure but in agnosticism. This is how

Sextus Empiricus described the process of finding the Sceptical path and stumbling on peace of mind:

> Now we shall deal with the *telos* of the Sceptical path.... We say again that the *telos* of the Sceptic is *ataraxia* in matters of belief and moderate feeling in matters which are unavoidable.
>
> He starts out in philosophy with a view to making decisions about sense impressions and grasping which are true and which are false, so as to attain *ataraxia*. But he encounters conflicts with equally strong arguments on both sides. He is unable to make decisions about these, and he suspends his judgement. When he suspends his judgement, the result, by lucky chance, is *ataraxia* in matters of belief.
>
> The man who thinks that things are good or bad by nature is constantly disturbed.... But the man who determines nothing concerning what is good or bad by nature neither flees nor pursues anything eagerly. He therefore experiences *ataraxia*. (*Outlines of Pyrrhonism*, 1.12)

On this view, *ataraxia* is a kind of lucky accident – something which the naïve seeker ends up finding by chance after he has tried looking for it in the wrong place. He starts out thinking that committing to one of the Dogmatic philosophies will bring him serenity, and ends up discovering that the opposite is the case.

Finally in this section, we may briefly take a closer look at Sextus' concept of "moderate feeling in matters which are unavoidable". Sextus went on to expand on this idea, and what he meant was essentially this. The Sceptic is not exempt from suffering the random vicissitudes of life. He will still get cold. He will still get thirsty. But his cold or thirst will not trouble him as much as it troubles an ordinary person. This is because the Sceptic will not add to the physical discomfort of those experiences by making a negative value judgement on them. It is bad enough to experience the unpleasant sensation of being cold without making things worse by getting annoyed about the *fact* that you are cold.

*

The Sceptical method of doing philosophy is to play off one's sense perceptions and one's intellectual opinions against themselves and against each other. The result is that the Sceptic succeeds in indefinitely putting off the point at which he has to arrive at a settled position on anything.

Scepticism was not a system and it laid down no rules. It had no Ten Commandments or Four Noble Truths. Nevertheless, ancient writers succeeded in summing up Sceptical ideas and methods in the form of several convenient lists. Each of these lists set out a series of what were termed "modes". These "modes" can be regarded as techniques for entering into the Sceptical mindset – gateways into serene indifference. The lists were not fixed or canonical: nothing in Scepticism was. Their contents and their order could differ from one version to another.

It will be useful to consider two of these lists of modes in a little more detail. We may start with the Five Modes of Agrippa. Agrippa was an obscure character who lived in the 1st or 2nd century AD. The Five Modes attributed to him are essentially tools which allow the

Sceptic to deconstruct Dogmatic arguments and reasoning. In principle, they can be used to destroy any claim about anything – or at least to reduce it to indifference.

The First Mode of Agrippa is Disagreement. If there is one thing that is certain in human affairs, it is that people will find some way of disagreeing about *anything*. This is clearly the case in philosophy – as shown by the very fact that we have opposing camps of Stoics, Epicureans and so on – but it is also evident in life more generally. Clever (and stupid) people can come up with good arguments for and against just about any proposition. We even do it as a recreational activity, as shown by the existence of debating clubs and internet "discussion" forums. As Sextus made clear in the passage quoted above, the Sceptical view is that the mass of conflicting, mutually exclusive claims about everything should have the effect of causing us to suspend judgement. How can any of us, as individuals, hope to resolve debates that have been raging for millennia? It is, incidentally, worth nothing that a committed Pyrrhonist would have to accept that in theory some issues *might* one day be decided conclusively – it just hasn't happened yet.

The Second Mode of Agrippa is Infinite Regress. This is an easy one. It draws on the fact that there are no uncontroversial, self-evident premises for believing anything. If you choose to claim that A is the case, you need to be able to justify that claim. So you point to B as evidence. But then you need to justify B... and so on until you give up and admit that maybe you don't really know anything at all. When children play the cheap trick of asking you "why?" in response to everything, they are applying the Second Mode of Agrippa. In practice, Dogmatists generally try to escape from Infinite Regress by resorting to either Hypothesis (the Fourth Mode) or Circularity (the Fifth Mode).

The Third Mode of Agrippa is Relativity. We can only regard A from a particular standpoint and a particular context. This means that we do not have the luxury of being able to make absolute, objective statements about A. The world doesn't look much like a sphere from where I'm standing, so I can entertain the possibility that it's really flat. What's more, you can't point me to the pictures taken from the Moon, because the mode of Disagreement tells me that some people claim that the Moon landings were a hoax. If you think that that's a flippant example, try this one instead. There is no such thing as racial or sexual discrimination in our society because I, a white man, have *never experienced either*.

The Fourth Mode of Agrippa is Hypothesis. A Dogmatist may seek to put a stop to Infinite Regress by positing some fundamental premise or "hypothesis". She might try to choose something so basic or self-evident that nobody could possibly disagree with it. But – as we have seen with the mode of Disagreement – someone can always be found to disagree with anything. The Epicurean tells the Sceptic that he at least ought to trust the evidence of his own senses. The Sceptic replies that maybe the Epicurean's senses are an illusion – and so is the rest of the world because the Epicurean is really a brain in a jar.

The Fifth Mode of Agrippa is Circularity. This is what happens when somebody tries to confirm A by reference to B in circumstances where B itself is dependent on A. How does devout old Auntie Lydia know that the Bible is the literal word of God? Because it claims quite clearly that it is; and the claim must be true because it appears in the literal word of God. We might smile when Auntie Lyds says this, but this simple example should not blind us to the fact that there are some very sophisticated ways of doing the same thing which can be quite difficult to spot.

So much for Agrippa's modes. As we noted, they can in principle be used to undermine any assertion about anything. In practice, we might find that different ones are effective to differing extents in inducing scepticism, depending on the actual situation at hand. They all work in theory, but not all of us are made of stern enough stuff to embrace things like NASA conspiracy theories or the brain in a jar thing.

A different set of Ten Modes was compiled by Aenesidemus. These may be seen as variations on the theme of the Third Mode of Agrippa, although the list was apparently devised earlier than Agrippa's. It seems that Agrippa went further in his Scepticism than Aenesidemus. The keynote of the Third Mode of Agrippa was Relativity; and the basic purpose of the Ten Modes of Aenesidemus is to encourage us to mistrust our perceptions of things by highlighting that they are inescapably relative. There is no neutral, authoritative standpoint from which we can view the world. This, argued the Sceptics, means that we should suspend judgement about everything. Not everyone will find that last link in the argument convincing – but bear with me while we review the Ten Modes.

The First Mode of Aenesidemus is based on the differences in perspective between different living creatures. To take a simple example, we know that not all animals can see the range of colours that we can see; while, conversely, some animals can hear sounds that are imperceptible to the human ear. The same principle can be extended to behaviour and morality. A cat who has successfully caught a mouse will perceive the situation differently from the mouse. He will approach it on the basis of a different set of value judgements. His owner will have a different perspective again and may think that mouse tastes disgusting anyway. Human perceptions are not the only perceptions in existence; and we cannot declare them to be authoritative, because we are parties to this conflict and we cannot be judges in our own cause. Maybe it's the cats who are objectively right.

The Second Mode of Aenesidemus is based on the differences, both physical and mental, between different human beings. These differences cause each of us to perceive things differently. Even if we could decide that the perceptions of humans are authoritative over those of (say) cats, we cannot say that the perceptions of any one human are authoritative over those of everybody else. I like the music of Richard Wagner; you prefer Lord Andrew Lloyd-Webber. Your outlook and career choices made you into a heroin trafficker; mine made me into the policeman who's about to nick you.

The Third Mode of Aenesidemus is based on differences between sense perceptions. Even if we could pick out a single human being – say, a philosophical guru like Zeno or Epicurus – and agree that his perceptions should be treated as authoritative, his own different senses would be inconsistent between themselves. After all, we have five senses and they quite often tell us different things. Our eyes may tell us that a painting is heavily textured, but it feels perfectly flat to the touch. Things that taste good may look unappetising. This mode is particularly threatening to philosophies like Epicureanism which embrace an empirical approach to the world. If we can't trust the evidence of our own senses, our reason has nothing reliable to act upon. We might as well not think anything at all.

The Fourth Mode of Aenesidemus is based on differences in perception due to personal circumstances. Let's say that we somehow manage to identify a perfectly trustworthy guru and isolate one of his senses as completely reliable. We still haven't solved our problem because he would not have – could *never* have – access to ideal, neutral circumstances in which to perceive things. This can easily be shown. An item of food might seem appealing to a person who is hungry but not to someone who is full up. A cup of wine might taste sweet to you if you have just eaten nuts, but sour if you have just eaten figs. Your attitude towards things will differ according to whether you are in mourning or you are ecstatically happy.

The Fifth Mode of Aenesidemus is based on differences in perceptions due to location. This is more of a basic, physical point, but it is equally inescapable. The sun looks small to us, but that's only because we're looking at it from a long way off. The light of a lamp looks dim when seen outdoors during the daytime, but bright when the lamp is lit in the depths of somebody's house after dark.

The Sixth Mode of Aenesidemus is based on "mixtures". This mode is rather obscure. The idea is that nothing affects our senses unless it is in *combination* with something else. The colour purple looks different depending on whether it is "mixed" with sunlight, moonlight or lamplight. The same noise will sound different depending on the acoustics of the space in which it is heard.

The Seventh Mode of Aenesidemus is based on differences in quantities and qualities. This is much easier to grasp. Your conclusions on the true nature of Scotch whisky may well differ depending on whether you drink a single measure of it or a bottle.

The Eighth Mode of Aenesidemus is based on relativity. I can only say that the table is on the right because of the position in which I happen to be sitting. In the same way, "father and brother are relative terms, day is relative to the sun, and all things are relative to our mind" (Diogenes Laertius, 9.88; trans. R.D.Hicks). This is a bit of a curious one. In his discussion of the Modes of Aenesidemus, Sextus Empiricus rightly observes that this mode really embraces all of the other nine. As we have noted, all ten of the Modes of Aenesidemus are concerned with relativity.

The Ninth Mode of Aenesidemus is based on rarity. Our perceptions in relation to X will differ according to how common or uncommon X is in our experience. Someone who lives in Surbiton might doubt the reality of earthquakes; but this is less likely for someone who lives on the San Andreas Fault.

The Tenth Mode of Aenesidemus is based on differences in social norms. We not only perceive things from a particular physical location, as the Fifth Mode has taught us, we perceive them from a particular cultural standpoint too. If you ask someone whether same-sex marriage is a good idea, you'll get a different answer depending on whether his cultural assumptions have been shaped by Greenwich Village or a village in Kashmir.

Such are the Ten Modes of Aenesidemus. When combined with the Five Modes of Agrippa, they provide us with a mental toolbox with which to deconstruct any claim which a Dogmatist might make or which we might be tempted to make to ourselves. Psychological self-help for a Sceptic consists of internalising the modes, together with any other similar techniques which we might come across. By this means, we will come to avoid falling into the error of believing things; and by so doing we will ease ourselves into the state of *ataraxia*.

*

Now it is time to consider the objections that might be made to the Sceptics' philosophy.

The first objection is a fairly obvious one, and it may well have occurred to you already. Sure, it's good to question things. It's also useful to be aware of our own subjectivity and to remember that we can't be absolutely certain that we're right about stuff. But there must come a point when we have to stop doubting and start believing – for purely practical reasons, apart from anything else. A person who takes the Sceptics' advice seriously and doubts *everything* has no means of living anything approaching a normal life. Not only is she incapable of making complex moral choices, she is incapable of having breakfast for fear that the cornflakes in her bowl aren't a cunningly disguised helping of rat poison. If we are unsure about every aspect of every situation, we are incapable of acting. We are paralysed. We might as well not bother getting out of bed in the morning (if it even *is* really morning).

This objection was well known in ancient times. There were stories about Pyrrho recklessly stepping out in front of oncoming traffic, walking off cliffs and getting into bother with dogs due to his refusal to form views about anything. It is said that his friends had to step in so as to keep him out of harm's way. A more disturbing story recounted that a man fell into a pond and Pyrrho ignored him and walked on by, leaving the poor guy to drown. Now, it may well be that none of these stories is true; but they do identify a real, perhaps fatal, weakness in the Sceptical position.

Just as Dogmatists were well practised at making this objection, the Sceptics were well practised at responding to it. In short, they denied the premise that you need to *believe* things – in the fullest sense of the word – in order to act. The Sceptic (they argued) is able to live a normal, functional life by following *appearances*. She can proceed on the basis of her involuntary impressions without falling into the error of claiming that she actually *knows* anything substantive. There is no contradiction in accepting basic input from one's senses while reserving suspension of belief for matters which are intellectual in nature and are not self-evident. A Sceptic who is caught outside in the depths of winter is not required to argue that it is neither hot nor cold: she is allowed to put on her coat. A Sceptic who eats some honey – which is itself a legitimate response to the impulse of hunger – is allowed to say that the honey tastes sweet. She just needs to refrain from asserting any philosophical claims about honey having the essential nature of sweetness.

There are other ways of making essentially the same argument. The Sceptic can act on the basis of what seems to be *reasonable* – or more reasonable than the alternative – without committing herself to believing it to be the right thing in principle. She can also follow her instinctive feelings and comply with social customs. This provides an answer to the charge that the Sceptic wise man would have no barrier to killing and eating his own father.

Whether or not these responses are adequate is a matter of opinion. They introduce qualifications and reserve cases which might be thought to weaken the essential force of Scepticism. The Sceptical counter-arguments might seem to come very close to saying that the Sceptic does in effect believe things: she just uses intellectual dodges and wordplay to avoid admitting it.

Another objection might be that Scepticism is highly relativistic. Many people would find the ethical consequences of this unacceptable. Note that the Sceptics did not necessarily claim that there is *no such thing* as good or evil. That is the sort of absolute statement that a Dogmatist would make. Their claim, rather, was that human beings cannot be *sure* that they can reliably identify things that may be good or evil. But this still looks uncomfortably close to relativism in the "bad" sense. What resources does it leave us with to refute the amoral attitude that (as Isaiah Berlin put it) "I am in favour of kindness and you prefer concentration camps"? A Sceptic is not required to consider both of those preferences to be valid, but he *is* required to accept that neither can be *rejected*. And that is surely a problem. It is one thing to be neutral between the hypothesis of a flat earth and the hypothesis of a spherical earth. It is silly, yes, but we might consider it to be worth the effort in order to achieve inner serenity. But would any of us want to live in a world in which, say, Nazi racial theories were entertained as acceptable, if unproven, hypotheses? Or the authenticity of the *Protocols of Zion* was treated as a matter of inconclusive debate? Is *that* likely to produce *ataraxia*?

The final objection is psychological in nature. Scepticism is a worldview based on doubt. For that reason, it was always destined to be a minority interest – just as were Stoicism and Epicureanism, each for their own reasons. Some people are comfortable with being steadfastly agnostic about everything. Some people no doubt find *ataraxia* as a result. But it is fair to say that most people don't fit this psychological profile. Most people seem to need to know things, or at least to *believe* things. As a species, we find it nearly as difficult to live without meaning as we do to live without food and drink.

Printed in Great Britain
by Amazon.co.uk, Ltd.,
Marston Gate.